Building Confidence and Self-Esteem

How to Have Unbreakable Self-Confidence, Overcome Self-Doubt and be Successful in Life

© **Copyright 2022 - All rights reserved.**

The content contained within this book may not be reproduced, duplicated, or transmitted without direct written permission from the author or the publisher.

Under no circumstances will any blame or legal responsibility be held against the publisher, or author, for any damages, reparation, or monetary loss due to the information contained within this book, either directly or indirectly.

Legal Notice:

This book is copyright protected. It is only for personal use. You cannot amend, distribute, sell, use, quote or paraphrase any part, or the content within this book, without the consent of the author or publisher.

Disclaimer Notice:

Please note the information contained within this document is for educational and entertainment purposes only. All effort has been executed to present accurate, up to date, reliable, complete information. No warranties of any kind are declared or implied. Readers acknowledge that the author is not engaging in the rendering of legal, financial, medical, or professional advice. The content within this book has been derived from various sources. Please consult a licensed professional before attempting any techniques outlined in this book.

By reading this document, the reader agrees that under no circumstances is the author responsible for any losses, direct or indirect, that are incurred as a result of the use of information contained within this document, including, but not limited to, errors, omissions, or inaccuracies.

Table of Contents

Introduction

Chapter One: Confidence and Self-Esteem

　Self-Confidence

　Self-Esteem

　Can You Have Self-Confidence but Not Self-Esteem?

　How It Affects You

　How to Boost Your Self-Esteem and Self-Confidence Levels

Chapter Two: Confidence and the Brain

　Confidence Originates in the Brain

　How Confidence Impacts Your Brain

　Three Techniques to Teach Your Brain to Improve Your Confidence

　How Do You Reprogram Your Mind?

Chapter Three: Freeing Yourself from Judgement

　Why do we Fear the Judgment of Others?

　How to Conquer the Fear of Being Judged

　Why Do We Think How Others Perceive Us Is Important?

Chapter Four: The Beauty of Mistakes, Why You Shouldn't Be Afraid of Making Them & How They Benefit You

　How to Not Be Scared of Failing

　Techniques to Stop Being Scared of Failure

Chapter Five: Stop Overthinking

　Recognize Your Triggers

Acknowledge the Things You Can Control and the Things You Can't

Delay and Diminish the Thoughts That Make You Anxious

Reprogram Your Brain to Concentrate on Certain Things Only

Why Do We Overthink At All?

Recognize and Welcome the Things You Are Scared Of

Chapter Six: Training to Be Confident

The Aspects of Being Confident

Learning the Ways to Build Confidence

Chapter Seven: Practicing with Purpose

Risks Are Good

Chapter Eight: The Key to Increasing Your Confidence

Understanding What You're Strong At

Understanding What Your Weaknesses Are

Why Is Understanding My Strengths and Weaknesses Important?

Is It Better to Concentrate Only on My Strengths or Just My Weak Points?

Chapter Nine: Looking the Part

Ways to Appear More Confident

Chapter Ten: Balancing between Confidence and Overconfidence

What Are the Differences between Confidence and Overconfidence?

Conclusion

Resources

Introduction

Being a functional adult in this day and age is nothing short of a colossal challenge. We have to juggle careers, personal growth, family, and health all in one go and somehow still be able to have time to reflect on ourselves. It's no easy feat by any means. Consequently, it's not very surprising that many of us struggle with introspection, and as a result, our self-esteem takes quite a hit. Whether it's from life experiences in the past or being overwhelmed in the present and uncertain about the future, there's always something contributing to an unstable and sometimes unhealthy self-image.

We hear the word confidence in many aspects of our day-to-day lives, but what does it really mean? Confidence is where you believe in yourself, that you have the belief in your abilities to overcome any obstacles that life throws your way and to be victorious in doing so. It also means you are willing to make decisions and see them through. In order to be confident, you will need to be able to understand and accept your abilities, work on your flaws, and feel assured of that understanding.

Showing you feel confident can allow you to gain integrity and trust in yourself, find ways of coping with pressure, make good impressions when meeting others for the first time, and look at obstacles – both personally and professionally – and find ways of overcoming them. Because confidence makes others around you feel safe and secure, it is also an extremely attractive characteristic.

Confidence also means that you are secure in your abilities and yourself. It is not to be confused with arrogance; it is more accurate, more assured. Confidence is not about whether you feel condescending or arrogant to those around you but rather the understanding that you can do what you need to do.

Those who have confidence feel secure instead of being doubtful. They depend on their knowledge and capabilities to overcome any obstacles instead of stopping, know they can take on whatever tests or challenges the day throws at them and say that they can instead of saying they cannot.

Why Confidence Matters

Confidence matters for numerous reasons, but the number one reason is preparing us for what life throws at our feet. When you feel confident, you can deal with others and whatever opportunities present themselves without being overwhelmed and backing away. Should it not work out on the first try, we have the confidence in ourselves to try once more.

However, when your confidence isn't quite as high, you may find it hard to talk to others or grab an opportunity with both hands. Unconfident people try something and fail, but instead of looking at what went wrong, they give up and don't want to try again.

You are less likely to meet your entire potential if you don't have enough confidence.

Look back on your life. When was the last time someone recognized a good quality in you? Maybe you are great at sports, writing novels, making art, and being creative with your hands. Maybe you're a shrewd business person, great at research; maybe your kindness knows no bounds?

Having someone recognize qualities or characteristics that we often ignore or don't see in ourselves can significantly boost our confidence levels. But this only works if we believe in ourselves as well. It's easy to doubt what other people say that they see in us, but this is not helpful and can be incredibly damaging to building confidence.

To be genuinely confident, you must be secure in the knowledge that you are competent. To get that knowledge, you need to use all your abilities and skills and continue to learn and exercise them.

When we start to build our confidence, we can step forward, allowing us to hone these skills. As we do so, we become proud of our achievements, taking our confidence to a new level.

Confidence is associated with nearly all aspects of a fulfilled and joyful life. There are so many benefits of being confident.

These include:

You Silence the Ugly Voices in Your Head

We've all been there. We have started to do something new, and that ugly little voice in the back of your head says to you: "you can't do this." That voice stops you from trying something new, not talking to a stranger, and not applying for that fantastic job you've dreamed of for years. That voice is your worst enemy. When you become confident, you will finally be able to silence that ugly little voice and take the next step forward.

When you are dealing with little to no confidence in yourself, you constantly ponder over mistakes you may have made, comments other people have said, or even things you wished you might have said. This is called rumination and is also associated with depression and anxiety. It has the annoyingly devastating effect of making you step away from your goals, sinking further into the shadows. But as your confidence levels begin to grow, you will be able to step out of the shadows and into the light.

To build up your levels of confidence, you need to start by accomplishing small goals or steps that you can look back upon feeling accomplished. If you speak another language, have a great experience with a skill, or overcome a significant hurdle, you've made the first step.

You may think to yourself that something small you accomplished ten years ago can't have any sort of positive impact on how you feel about yourself today. However, this could not be further from the truth.

Look back at that time – how much work, effort, and time did it take you to achieve it? If you could do it ten years ago, nothing would stop you from putting that same work, effort, and time into something else today.

You will discover that your drive to learn and grow more will increase as you build up your confidence. You may still hear that ugly little voice in the back of your head saying, 'what if,' but they won't be as damaging as they were. Instead, you will tell that voice to shut up and feel invigorated and empowered as you continue to reach one goal after the other.

Setbacks, obstacles, failures ... these are all aspects of life that you can't escape from at some time or another. However, being confident in yourself will allow you to understand that even though you may fail at times, you do have the ability to learn from them and try again instead of falling down and not getting back up. If things don't work out as you plan, confidence in yourself will stop you from berating and belittling yourself.

Failures Are Good Things

In fact, failures and setbacks are a fantastic way of growing your confidence and not letting it develop into arrogance. When you try something new – maybe a new job, living overseas, studying for a new degree, etc. – you will have times of success and times of failure. Failing at something allows you to understand what you did wrong and accept that it's just something you have to deal with. After all, no one is perfect!

What is ironic is that if you are willing to fail, you will be more successful. This is because you understand and accept that not everything goes by your plans, nor does everything need to be perfect before starting. You can't score a goal if you never kick the ball!

It may feel strange but having confidence in yourself means you don't concentrate on yourself as much. For example, say you put on a new outfit and walk into a room. You may think that everyone looks at you and believe you look hideous. But the truth of the matter is no one thinks that except for you. Other people are more concerned with the things that are going on in their own lives. Those negative thoughts stop you from fully connecting with other people.

When you stop focusing on negativity, you will begin to like engaging with others much more than before simply because you're not anxious or afraid of what they think of you. You start to understand that it's not a competition and you don't need to compare yourself to them. They will feel this relaxation and confidence and become less anxious about themselves and you, allowing you to build stronger relationships.

Developing New Emotions

Being confident in yourself also helps you develop empathy. When your head isn't inundated with negativity and chaotic thoughts, you will notice if your friend looks upset or if your date looks worried. It allows you to lend a hand to others and say, "do you need help?"

Who You Are

As you start to live a life of confidence, you will begin to discover who you truly are. You start to see your weak points, accept them, and understand that they don't lower your worth. Not only that, but you continue to draw on your strengths in order to get to where you want to be.

You discover what means the most to you in life, what principles and ethics you believe in, and what you will fight for.

Twelve Things Genuinely Confident People Do

There are many forms of confidence, ranging from arrogance to not saying anything at all. Many people fake confidence to the world, wearing a mask so that no one sees their fears and insecurities beneath it, but genuine confidence requires no mask at all.

Those who are confident in their skills, capabilities, and knowledge will always be at least three steps ahead of others since they tend to be inspirational and make opportunities arise.

You can or can't – the choice is yours, and yours alone.

What you believe you are capable of doing – and what you're not capable of doing – is entirely down to you. Your mind will get you to where you want to be, and studies at many universities all around the world prove this.

To be confident, you must learn how to be confident. So, what do genuinely confident people do that insecure people don't?

i. They Are Happy with Themselves

There are many aspects of confidence, and happiness is one of them. To be genuinely confident, you must genuinely accept and be happy with yourself. Confident people take pride and happiness in their accomplishments, not how others see their achievements. They understand that they are not the person others see, and that's absolutely fine.

ii. They Don't Judge Others

Those who are genuinely confident do not judge other people. This is because they know not everyone has the same starting point in life and that everyone is struggling with something that most people don't know about. They understand they don't have to step on other people's dreams and goals to feel secure in their own. When you compare yourself to others, it limits you and your goals and is a waste of time and energy.

iii. They Don't Agree with Everything

Universities in the United States of America have shown that people who are not confident to say no have increased risks of depression, anxiety, burning out, and stress. Being able to say no to someone or something is a healthy thing to do, and confident people are well aware of this. Those with genuine confidence will not say "I don't know," or "I am not sure"; they say, "This doesn't work for me," or "No, thank you," confidently as they are aware that they have existing commitments that they need to finish before starting a new one.

iv. Confident People Listen More

People often start rambling on and on simply because they feel that they will lose their courage to see something through if they stop talking. It's a way of them trying to prove to themselves that they can do it. However, genuinely confident people know that they don't have to do this, allowing them to listen to other people and focus on engaging with them, leading to a much more fulfilling and successful style.

v. Confident People Talk with Conviction

If you hear the words 'I'm not sure" or "I believe so" or "maybe," it doesn't fill you with confidence. It makes you doubt their abilities or timeframe. Genuinely confident people talk with conviction as they are aware of two things; one, they know they can get it done, and two, they know people won't be assured of their abilities if you're not assured of your own abilities.

vi. They Understand the Importance of Small Goals

It's well known that confident people enjoy challenges and competitions, no matter how big or small the victories are. Accomplishing smaller goals produces more androgen receptors in sections of the brain associated with purpose and incentives. The more androgen receptors in the brain, the more testosterone is produced, resulting in higher levels of confidence to deal with more situations later on. These chemical reactions can be experienced for several months at a time, even if the accomplishments are small.

vii. Exercising Helps

Exercising is fantastic for building up your confidence. A Canadian university discovered that people who regularly exercised for ten weeks felt more confident in several areas, including athletically, through their studies, and within society. Although many of them saw changes physically, it was actually the endorphins released through an exercise that caused the boost in their confidence.

viii. They Don't Go Looking for Attention

Have you ever seen someone who just lives for drama? Every week it's something new? Do you find it attractive? Nope. It's off-putting, to say the least. Genuinely confident people do not go looking for attention. They are well aware that it is better for them and everyone else if they are themselves and not trying to prove anything.

Confident people can also divert attention away from themselves and put the spotlight on everyone who helped with it. For example, a confident boss celebrating an accomplishment will shine the spotlight on every single person in their team that helped achieve it. They don't seek everyone's praise for themselves because they already know and understand their worth inside.

ix. They Accept When They Are Wrong

Genuinely confident people know that when they make mistakes, they accept them. Many times, they believe something and are truly grateful when someone else proves otherwise. This is because they discover something about themselves when proven wrong and learn something about the other person. They know it's nothing personal.

x. They Grab Opportunities

Have you ever been offered an opportunity that you wished you'd taken but feared held you back from grabbing it? Genuinely confident people don't listen to the ugly voices in the back of their heads – or the negative things other people say – they grab those opportunities and don't let go. Even if they are scared about what could happen, they put their butts on the line and just go for it since they know there is something to learn through both failures and successes.

xi. They Recognize Greatness in Others

People with low self-confidence will normally try to hog the limelight or put down other people to prove themselves. However, genuinely confident people don't stress over the limelight or feel the need to prove anything because they value their own internal worth. Instead, they focus outwardly, giving them the chance to recognize the greatness and potential of others around them and verbalize this to those people.

xii. They're Not Scared to Admit They Need Help

No one is perfect. Not all skills are perfect. But unlike unconfident people, those who are sure of themselves know that when they need help, they can ask for it without losing face, looking weak, or appearing incompetent. They recognize their strengths, what their weaknesses are, and if there are gaps that others can help them fill in. In addition, they understand that asking for help from someone who has more skills and experience gives them the chance to grow and develop their own skills for the future.

Chapter One:
Confidence and Self-Esteem

The terms self-confidence and self-esteem are regularly exchangeable with each other despite the fact that they have genuinely different meanings.

Self-confidence is the term used to calculate how much we believe in our abilities. Self-esteem is the term used to measure how much we believe in ourselves and our interactions with our surroundings. The two meanings can often make people confused and lead them to increase their self-esteem through skills and accomplishments.

Self-Confidence

The term self-confidence is related to your beliefs concerning certain aspects of your life, how much you trust yourself and your skills to accomplish aspirations, and your successes at overcoming obstacles. Self-confidence can be described as looking outwards and tends to be simpler to achieve in comparison to self-esteem. Self-confidence originates in ability and training, which is why the more you do things, the more confident you feel when doing them. The word originates from the term fidere, which means 'to trust' in Latin. As such, to become confident, you must trust in yourself and your abilities with the rest of the world. Generally, confidence in yourself results in success, which carries on building more confidence. Despite this, many people try to build up their self-esteem through self-confidence, which does not work in the long run, as it only lasts when you succeed at new challenges.

Self-Esteem

Self-esteem describes our feelings about ourselves and impacts how we think, how we feel, and what actions we take. Self-confidence is about facing outward, self-esteem refers to facing inwards, which impacts how you interact with people and the rest of the world. It originates from aestimare, the Latin term which translates as 'to appraise,' referring to how much you appraise your own worth. It is shaped via the experiences you have in life along with your relationships with people. Those with healthy levels of self-esteem don't feel the need to use how much they earn or what material possessions they have to feel worthy or are scared of rejection or not succeeding. They understand and accept all experiences, both negative and positive, and accept others for who they are.

Can You Have Self-Confidence but Not Self-Esteem?

Just because the terms are often interchangeable doesn't mean that they always go hand in hand. Sometimes, you may have low self-esteem but high levels of self-confidence. For example, an author may have confidence in their abilities to write fantastic novels but then suffer from lower self-esteem levels and not believe they are worthy of success.

Despite this, it is common that as you work on one area, such as raising your self-confidence, you actually increase your self-esteem.

Many people discover that it is much simpler to work on increasing their levels of self-confidence instead of their self-esteem. Because of this, the result is a large list of skills and accomplishments. Instead of actually looking in a mirror, recognizing and accepting their mistakes, and working on them, they cower behind credentials and what they've earned. However, in the real world, just because you have a certificate or prize doesn't mean that you have good, healthy levels of self-esteem.

People with self-confidence trust themselves and their abilities to interact with others effectively or productively with the rest of the world. When new obstacles emerge in their paths, they can seize the opportunity, take responsibility when things go wrong, and learn from it all. Some people discover that they are confident in particular areas, for example, writing, singing, and dancing, but are not confident in others, such as marketing, cooking, or relationships.

When there is little or no confidence, it is time to be brave. Confidence is the trust you have in your known abilities, whereas bravery is that of the things you don't know. For example, if you have experience in public speaking, then you know you can talk in front of a live audience, yet if you have no experience, you may not be confident in your abilities to do the same. There is incredible strength in doing something you have never done compared to doing something you have done.

Those with good, healthy self-esteem levels don't require external stimuli to feel good about themselves. Things such as drugs, money, sex, and status are nothing to them. They trust and respect themselves, maintaining their health and surroundings. They participate in others and projects completely, not fearing rejection or failure. As with every other human on Earth, they experience pain and disappointment, but these are just obstacles for them to overcome. They are resilient, growing with each new experience and relationship, understand and accept risks, and forgive themselves and others when mistakes are made.

How It Affects You

A lot of people suffer from low self-esteem levels or low levels of self-confidence. Sometimes they only apply to certain aspects of life, yet it can be extremely devastating or controlling for some.

If you suffer from low self-confidence or self-esteem, if you look back in your life, you may be able to trace it back to a particularly negative experience that has gone on to shape how you view yourself. It can create never-ending cycles of negativity that will continue unless you break your way of thinking.

For example, you write a book and send it off to an agent to be considered for publication. A few months later, you receive a letter from the agent saying that they won't be considering it at this time. You may think to yourself that you're dumb, that you have no skills, and you shouldn't try again.

If someone with healthy self-esteem gets the same response, they ask what they need to do to improve the manuscript or what mistakes were made to achieve a better outcome the next time they submit it. Feeling disappointment is perfectly natural; just don't let it stop you from improving and moving forward.

Being shy, having difficulty communicating with others, feeling anxious around social situations, and not being assertive enough are all signs of low self-confidence. Having a loud fault-finding voice within yourself that becomes louder when you start feeling exhausted, anxious, or that others are judging you are signs of low self-esteem.

When you listen to that inner critic, you start thinking that all the negative things it tells you are true. You believe that you overlook all your assets and skills, you believe that everything you do will fail, and start avoiding circumstances that will test you or where you think others will judge you and believe that you're not meant to have fun or that you don't deserve to.

When you start believing in that annoyingly ugly voice, you start to place limitations on your life in numerous ways, not just in your studies or career, but also in communicating with others and negatively affecting your relationships.

How to Boost Your Self-Esteem and Self-Confidence Levels

Now that you understand the differences between self-confidence and self-esteem and how they interact with each other, you can start boosting your levels and fulfilling your potential.

Learn to Accept Yourself

When you start to accept yourself – flaws and strengths alike – you start to believe in yourself, your abilities, and who you are as a person and feel good about others no matter the circumstances. Everyone makes mistakes, and everyone fails, but when you learn to accept yourself, you realize that mistakes are a way for you to learn and grow, to recognize new ways to problem solve, and recognize the flaws you have in an attempt to change them but not being harsh on yourself.

Discover Who You Are

Finding out who you really are as a person can positively affect your self-confidence and self-esteem levels. Recognize what strengths you have, what abilities you possess, and what you have accomplished. Be proud of everything, regardless of how big or small it is. Ask yourself why these are important and what aspects you want to improve.

Change How You Think

It's very easy not to think about how you talk to yourself or what things you say. For most, we are actually kinder to others than to ourselves. When your inner voice starts talking, start challenging them. Pay attention to the positive things and ignore the negative comments. Changing how you think will change everything for you.

Stand Up for Yourself

Being assertive isn't rude or wrong. It's so easy to ignore your wants or needs, especially with others, but learn to stand up for yourself and say what you truly want. It's nothing to be guilty or ashamed of.

Implement Changes

Making a change – or several – can drastically impact your self-confidence and self-esteem. Decide on the areas you want to change or improve in order, then make the necessary arrangements. If you're unhappy in your workplace, you may want to look for a new job, a career change, or learn new skills.

How to do this? Easy –

1. *Write down the goals you want to achieve*
2. *Divide every goal into smaller steps*
3. *Achieve one small step at a time*

Another good thing to do is to get rid of all the toxic people in your life. People who are constantly whining or critical can easily have a negative effect on your life.

Celebrate Each Accomplishment

No matter how small you think the accomplishment is, it is still a success! Each accomplishment helps you to raise your self-confidence and esteem. Make sure you celebrate each one.

Chapter Two:
Confidence and the Brain

Being confident is attractive to many people and is usually something most want more of. People pay attention to those who speak clearly and confidently or make the decisions no one else has. Being confident gives you that quality that generally results in success in various elements of life, such as having a fantastic career, a healthy relationship, or maintaining your mental health.

Confidence Originates in the Brain

Scientists have believed for quite some time that the orbitofrontal cortex, known as the OFC, impacts confidence. This part of the brain is associated with the cognitive method of making decisions and is also believed to play an important role in our emotions. We know that it is also associated with the limbic system, which is linked to memories and emotions. A study shows that when neurons were switched off in the OFC in rats, they showed a lower rate of confidence-induced decisions. Although these subjects were rats, scientists are confident that the human brain is affected the same way.

Other studies showed that sections of the brain associated with assessment and learning experienced errors and changes when self-esteem levels were lowered. In simple terms, a person's self-esteem can change based on the way they perceive how others like and value them, in turn affecting their learning ability.

How Confidence Impacts Your Brain

When you start to experience positive thoughts, you start up the area of the brain that is associated with happiness, motivation, and incentive, which then causes you to feel good. This means that your levels of self-confidence improve when you start reprogramming your brain to think positively.

The brain is easily shaped, which means it is easier to train than you may initially think. However, your levels of self-confidence and self-esteem can be affected by past experiences, health issues, and your surroundings. It is important that you recognize the impact that each of these, and others, has on you as you move forward.

Three Techniques to Teach Your Brain to Improve Your Confidence

Low self-confidence can lead to numerous difficulties in your life. As such, it is important to teach your brain and reprogram it to ensure more positivity as you move forward.

i. Stop Comparing Yourself to Other People

It's easy to compare your work, skills, and entire being to someone else. A quick thought, and bam! You're sobbing in a corner, asking yourself why you ever started. This negative thinking trains your brain to constantly think negatively, causes you anxiety, and then impacts how well you perform, which, when put together, drastically impacts your confidence. Don't see them as someone to compete with, but rather someone who can teach you things.

ii. Concentrate on Your Actions Rather Than the Results

Concentrate on what you have to do to get the outcome you want instead of the outcome itself to feel good about yourself. Reprogram your mind to be positive without seeing the outcome first.

iii. Recognize Your Self-Doubt as Signs

Doubting your abilities or capabilities is a sign of an underlying cause. However, this means that it can increase your confidence when you start to address and work on them. When these doubts start to surface, question yourself about what you want and what you need. Look where these things are occurring and where they aren't. What seems to be the case for many people is that the aspects of your life or being that make you feel unconfident are the parts where your needs aren't being fulfilled.

While these three aspects are the biggest things to work on, you can also train your brain by enhancing your cognitive skills, including logic, memory, and attention skills.

Although the subconscious part of our brains takes in information and assumptions while we are young, it lacks the capability to justify it. Think of it as a record player, spinning information around and around, playing the assumptions with each turn.

Every day, we constantly talk to ourselves, and the brain responds with things that will go on to affect how we see and interact with the world. People with low self-esteem or confidence will hear negative messages, saying that they're not strong, ugly, or not smart enough. The good news is you can reprogram your brain through positive affirmations.

Before you do that though, you need to recognize when you're telling yourself negative messages. Be honest and logical in this step. If you don't feel confident when speaking to those in a higher position than you, your inner critic might tell you that you're not intelligent enough or you don't have the power to say no to them no matter what.

The scary thing about the brain is that whatever you feed it, it will return it to you in multiples. So, if you constantly berate yourself by saying that you don't hold any value or strengths, that you're worthless, then your brain will reinforce that thinking, which will taint everything you experience. Don't be alarmed at this, though, because now you are aware of it; you can make the changes to reprogram your mind.

How Do You Reprogram Your Mind?

Once you recognize that your experiences are based on your own thoughts, you recognize that you have the power to change them.

You don't need to figure out where, when, and how the negative inner critic first appeared to reprogram your mind. The main aspect of brain training is through affirmations. This is where you repeat positive messages, constantly on repeat, until it wipes out the negative statements.

One way of doing this is starting a journal. Write down all the negative things you tell yourself that trigger your self-doubts. Next, write down all your affirmations, the statements that you silence your inner critic with. Repeat these statements several times throughout the day.

For example:

Negative: *I am not good enough.*

Affirmation: I have the tools to be successful.

Negative: *No one loves me.*

Affirmation: I am beautiful and kind.

You may find it helpful to write them down and place them in the places you spend time in, such as your office, your living room, the bathroom mirror, etc.

You can say them out loud when you're alone or repeat them in your head. They should be short, positive, and life-changing. Don't say 'I will'; say 'I am' as this cements you in the present, whereas the brain tends to put off future things.

Chapter Three:
Freeing Yourself from Judgement

Many of us feel as though the people around us are judging us. This could be friends, family members, colleagues, or even strangers on the street. It can be consuming and prevent you from interacting the way you want to with others or sharing positive things. However, when you stop caring about how other people think of you, you give yourself the gift of freedom.

It's not easy to free yourself from the judgment of others. There are times when the way you perceive how others see you stops you from doing the things you want to. In other cases, you might look at another person and start judging their actions. The truth is you are judging them because you would criticize yourself if you were in their shoes.

Judgment is where you determine the worth of something, whether positive or negative. It is a sad fact of life, but we are constantly being judged and constantly judging, which prevents us from genuinely interacting with others and our surroundings and appreciating their wonders. We determine everything which happens without our lives through our own beliefs. Even if we see and hear the same things as the person next to us does, our judgment will be different due to our individual experiences and insights. This includes how we see and treat ourselves.

Around ninety percent of our determinations don't serve any purpose. In fact, they are more likely to harm us. When you constantly spend time judging, analyzing, or labeling something, you start to cause chaos within your mind. You create your own suffering through negative thinking and emotions since judgment originates from uncertainty, fear, stress, and rage.

Sometimes in your life, you will find someone judging you for something. Everyone has the potential to be hurt by the negative words or actions of someone else. It can make you feel scared and defenseless that you will be judged harshly sometime down the road. This fear of others judging you affects how you look at opportunities, careers, friendships, and even relationships.

When we are kids, we don't fear what others think of us. As we get older, we start becoming more conscious of how we are perceived.

Why do we Fear the Judgment of Others?

There are many reasons why we get scared. For some, standing out from the crowd can be scary. If everyone is going right, but you're the only one who wants to go left, it can be scary to be the only one going that way.

When we are criticized for something we say, an feel like we're personally being y if that person is someone you admire or think is better than you. Otherwise, it would simply be their individual opinion, and you wouldn't see it as something true.

Having little or no support from the people we love and care about, such as friends and family members, can negatively affect how we look at ourselves.

Dark phases in our lives – maybe a relationship breakdown, the loss of a job, a traumatic event, etc. – can make us feel stripped of our shields and leave us more open and susceptible to the negative judgments of others.

It is a sad fact of life that society judges us for everything and anything. From a young age, we are constantly told to study more, to be thin, to be pretty, to be strong, in order to be accepted and loved by society. We are taught that to be loved, to be appreciated, and to belong, we must act certain ways or be rejected, thus programming us to obey.

How to Conquer the Fear of Being Judged

Boost Your Self Confidence

Raise the levels of regard you have in life in order to be fairer when being judged. Remember not to take things as an attack on you personally.

Be Clear of What You Want

When you are passionate and fulfilled in life, it tends to block out the judgments of other people. By focusing on improving yourself and being clear in what you want, you realize that the opinions of others can't stop you.

Have a Support Team

Having a good support system that constantly encourages and appreciates you can positively affect your confidence and esteem, making you feel stronger in your capabilities.

Why Do We Think How Others Perceive Us Is Important?

We've asked ourselves why we fear how others perceive us and how to conquer that fear, but why are other people's perceptions of us important?

As humans, we are sociable creatures, and feeling as though we belong somewhere is part of our nature. This means that we are socially conditioned to follow crowds and fear standing apart from them. When the people around us start judging us for not conforming, it can make you feel scared and anxious.

Read on for methods to conquer your fear of being judged.

- **Listen to Your Inner Critic**

Everyone has different sections of themselves. You have voices that say positive things that encourage you, and then you have a voice that says negative things that make you think others are judging you. Recognize them both and start controlling which one you listen to.

- **Recognize Your Strengths and Acknowledge Your Limitations**

If you know what areas you are good at, then it helps you to understand what limits you possess. Everyone has both but having confidence in your capabilities and recognizing your weak areas will serve you well. You can't be affected negatively if someone judges you to be bad at something you already know and accept. Take pride in your strengths and accomplishments, accept the things you're not strong in, and accept that they don't determine your worth. As time goes on, other people's opinions of you won't affect you.

- **Recognize When You're Being Judgmental**

We all make judgments about others at some time in our lives. It's only human nature, but you need to realize that when you are judging someone else, you are doing to them what you fear others are doing to you. That person could be scared of you judging them. As the old saying goes, you never know what struggles someone is going through. As you become mindful of your own judgments and reduce them, you become less caring about the judgments others make of you.

- **Make Time to Look after Yourself.**

Your number one priority in life should be yourself. You must care for and nurture yourself. You can do this in several ways: maintain a healthy diet and exercise, learn a new language or skill, read more books, practice mindfulness, or simply pamper yourself. Life can be stressful, especially if you're worried about how others view you, so it is important you take time to concentrate on your own well-being.

Chapter Four:
The Beauty of Mistakes, Why You Shouldn't Be Afraid of Making Them & How They Benefit You

Everyone makes mistakes; it's what makes us human. However, it is so easy to think of them as the start of failing at something due to no talent or skills. When you make a mistake, it's easy to start to feel negative, hopeless, and worthless. Yet, research shows that this is not the case – that mistakes are positive elements.

Researchers at Stanford University have shown that when you make a mistake, it is a fantastic opportunity to learn and grow. For example, you are attempting to build a new rocket ship to send to Mars, but the electronic motherboard doesn't work at certain pressures. This makes you look at what the pressure is doing to the motherboard and how to fix it. In your brain, fresh synaptic connections are formed, making it work and grow.

Research has also shown that surroundings where you make lots of mistakes actually allow for improved education, resulting in better perceptions and understanding.

People tend to fear making mistakes because they are associated with negativity, which then results in fear of trying again or attempting something new. Making a mistake can be something to dread, but fear is a good thing, according to scientists, as it indicates that you are continuing to grow. If you don't fear something, you stagnate. As such, you should embrace fear.

Everyone makes mistakes, but only a small percentage of people will actually see them for what they are: an opportunity to grow and learn. This is what makes great people, well, great. They accept their mistakes and use them as exercises in pushing for greatness.

- **Mistakes Mean New Chances**

When you make a mistake, you gift yourself the chance to illustrate what management skills you have. Don't try to hide them; use them to show your character and management skills.

- **They Increase Your Intelligence**

When you make a mistake, you have a choice, whether you berate and beat yourself up for it or to figure out what you did wrong. Those who do the latter show they are more likely not to make the same mistake again as they pay more attention and use their new understanding to increase their chances to learn and perform.

- **You Learn Quicker**

Scientists have discovered that when you are learning a new skill or activity, the brain actually learns faster and easier from making mistakes than just the activity.

- **They Improve Your Memory**

Scientists have discovered that when you make a mistake and try again later on, you avoid making it twice because your brain remembers it better. As a result, your memory improves.

- **Mistakes Are Motivational**

Researchers at a California university state that people who did not pass their exams but were more motivational and compassionate with themselves went on to spend longer preparing for the next test. In comparison, those who were negative about themselves after failing were less likely to be motivated to prepare.

- **Mistakes Can Reprogram Your Mind**

British psychologists have found that your mind will warn you just before you are about to make the same mistake twice.

- **Obtain Clear Vision**

Since we were young, older generations have told us that mistakes only happen when we do something wrong. However, when we look at our actions and how we got there, we obtain clarity, something we may not have had before attempting it. It also gives us the chance to determine our own definition of success. When you make a mistake, you can use it as an opportunity to help you get back on the path you want.

- **It Helps You Address Your Fears**

Society teaches us that mistakes are bad, and as a result, many of us are scared of making them. Pride is stronger than fear, and when our egos are vulnerable to something, we start to fear it. However, when you admit you've made a mistake and try to fix it, you are addressing your fears, allowing you to grow and develop.

- **You Show How Brave You Really Are**

When you face your fears, accept them, and try to fix them, it shows incredible bravery that many don't have. It is brave to admit to yourself that you aren't perfect, and even though the first attempt didn't work out, you are willing to try again.

- **Mistakes Are Inspirational**

When you make a mistake, it allows you to look at different routes and ideas. You have to look at how you initially approached it and find another way. When you make a mistake, you are taught what does not work, allowing you to find other ways to accomplish it. Your mind becomes more creative.

- **You Show Integrity**

Huge mistakes generally begin as small ones. Every choice you make will eventually add up, and you must be considerate of the integrity of those decisions. When mistakes are made, they can indicate that what you are doing is not in order. Therefore, you can look at your objectives, think about what is important, and make the necessary changes.

- **They Are Educational to Other People**

Mistakes are valuable teaching examples to those around us. Everyone is looking to improve themselves, to figure out what is going wrong in their projects. They will be inspired when you admit your mistakes to others and show them that you are trying to fix them. Leaders lead through example, and our mistakes can be educational for those going through the same thing.

How to Not Be Scared of Failing

Anyone with self-confidence and self-esteem knows that there is always the possibility of failure whenever we attempt anything, especially if it is new. When you accept that and welcome it, you are not just brave but giving yourself the chance to have a full and rewarding life.

If you are scared of potentially failing, there are some things you can do:

- **Calculate all the possible results**.

Not knowing the outcome of something can be powerfully scary for many. You can reduce this fear by thinking of all the outcomes that could happen if you only try.

- **Reprogram your mind to be more positive**.

If you're only thinking negatively – "I'm not good enough to succeed, so I'm not even going to try," or "oh, I'm not attractive enough to date them, so I'm not going to ask them out," your brain will think negatively every time a new experience presents itself. When you start thinking positively, you build up your self-confidence and self-esteem, making you look at new experiences differently.

- **Consider the worst**.

There will be times when the worst possible outcome actually occurs, and it is only natural to be scared of it. However, there are times when the worst outcome isn't quite as terrible as you first thought, and when you realize this, you're not quite as scared.

- **Have a backup plan**.

If you are really scared of failure, there is nothing wrong with having a backup plan. It can be comforting and reassuring if you do.

Techniques to Stop Being Scared of Failure

Establishing a series of goals can be a great technique to help you stop being scared of failure. Many experts agree that visualization is a fantastic way of setting goals, which will motivate you to push on.

However, visualization doesn't work with everyone. For some with low self-confidence and esteem issues, visualization techniques can make them feel dejected.

If this is the case for you, you may want to start setting one or two tiny goals to set you on the right path. These goals should be challenging enough but will not overwhelm you.

For example, you want a promotion at your job, and the person who can make it happen is someone who intimidates you. So, in this case, you should challenge yourself to go to their office and say hello. It's a small step on a ladder that will eventually take you to the top, but you can't get there until you put your foot on it.

Chapter Five:
Stop Overthinking

Anyone who overthinks knows exactly what happens. Something happens, such as a negative interaction with a colleague, and your mind stays fixed on it. You try to get your mind elsewhere, but it constantly comes back to what that person said to you.

It's so easy to constantly think about the issues and dilemmas we face, but this only leads to more stress, insomnia, lack of concentration, and low energy levels. Combined, it can make you feel sick, and if you don't find a way out of this horrendous cycle, you may develop depression.

There are methods you can implement to relax and stop overthinking, although there are some that appear positive on the surface but can actually do more harm than good.

Always looking out for danger. It's perfectly acceptable to be on the lookout for dangerous situations, but taking it too far can be incredibly damaging. For example, it's OK to be mindful of crossing the road, but if you're so worried that you can't leave your house without being scared of being run over, then it hasn't served you well.

Constantly looking for assurance. Sometimes we need assurance from others that we respect or admire. However, this is a troubling path if you're constantly worrying and stressing about not being good enough and keep asking others for their advice.

Constantly making plans. Making plans is great. It's healthy to have a calendar that you can remind yourself of things you need to do, deadlines to meet, or events to go to. However, it can become damaging when you plan the smallest details. Not only does this take up a lot of time, but it can also exaggerate existing fears or stresses.

Recognize Your Triggers

Scientists believe that the human mind creates thousands of memories, identifications, and thoughts on a daily basis. Most of these arrive and disappear without much notice, yet some stay with us for much longer. These are what experts call 'trigger thoughts'; if you concentrate on them long enough, they trigger many emotions and connotations.

Some of these can be positive: a doll your grandmother gave you years ago that you still keep in your closet, a brochure reminding you of an upcoming trip, or a reminder that you're going out with friends later that night – these give off waves of enjoyment and happiness, and will serve you well. Other trigger thoughts, such as 'what if...' or 'why don't they like me?' can cause negativity and could transform into stress and anxiety.

Trigger thoughts are similar to buses as you're waiting at the bus depot. Buses arrive and then depart to different places. In this, each bus represents a thought. If you jump onto the 'what if I'm not good enough?' station, then you could find yourself at another depot with the 'I can't do that,' 'I shouldn't even try,' and 'what's the point of even going?' buses. Or you can decide that the 'I can't do that' bus is not one you want to be on and simply let it go past you.

Trigger thoughts can be overwhelming and possibly lead to various issues (such as insomnia, stress, depression, etc.), but only if you allow them to be. Every single person around the world has trigger thoughts, but they only become troublesome when you decide to hop onto that bus and stay on it. The longer you stay on that bus, the more issues it will cause. The longer you dwell on a negative trigger thought, the more issues arise because of it.

Acknowledge the Things You Can Control and the Things You Can't

If you are someone who is constantly hopping onto buses – or spending too much time dwelling on those trigger thoughts – then you have formed a harmful pattern. If you continue dwelling on these trigger thoughts each time they pop up, it will become instinctive for your brain to linger on them. When this happens, you may think that you can't control it.

Trigger thoughts can't stop from popping up, and you don't have any say in which buses decide to stop at your bus depot. However, it is entirely down to you which bus you decide to get on. No, you can't control what trigger thoughts your brain sends your way, but it's your choice whether you pay them any attention and for how long. It's your choice to acknowledge them and move on, or to pay them more attention even though you know it will not be for your best benefit.

Thoughts are transitory. They come and go more than kids running in and out of the house. Think about what you did yesterday. How many thoughts did you have that you can recall right now? We have several thousand each day, but most people will only recall maybe half a dozen. This is because you don't pay the majority of them any special attention. We simply acknowledge them and get back to other things. You have the capability to do this with your trigger thoughts just as you do with the other thoughts.

Delay and Diminish the Thoughts That Make You Anxious

The majority of people who overthink find it hard to imagine that they are the ones in control of their thoughts. It's OK if you don't find these words convincing. A good way of testing this is by looking at ways to delay and diminish the thoughts that make you feel stressed and anxious. Some experts recommend only giving yourself a set time and length of time where you can worry without any constrictions, say between 18:30 to 19:00 each night. For example, it's 10:00 on a Monday morning, and you're at work when you suddenly experience a trigger thought regarding a test for the following week. Instead of dwelling on it right then and there, try to delay it until 18:30 by telling yourself that this is not the right time to think about such things and you'll concentrate on it later. You can do this same technique with things you feel you need assurance with.

> ***Side Note:*** *if you find it hard to sleep when you're overthinking something, you may want to do this a few hours before you go to bed.*

There are several fantastic benefits of setting aside a period of time for free worrying. First, it gives you the opportunity to challenge and test your beliefs that you are not in control of your trigger thoughts. Experts all around the world have discovered that many patients can delay their worries and actually are already doing it with other thoughts (such as terrifying events recorded in the news that you postpone reading about until later) or overhearing something at another desk that causes you stress, but then you focus your concentration back to your work. These are just two ways that illustrate that you're in control of every one of your thoughts, trigger thoughts or not, as well as how you deal with them.

Secondly, you learn that thoughts are fleeting and change constantly. For example, you're an author, and you experience thought in the morning about a new plot twist or character to introduce. However, several hours later, it doesn't seem important enough to note it down. Or you're on the way to work when you grab a breakfast meal to eat at your desk. However, it's too salty, and you decide to take it back later on and ask for a refund. At the end of the day, it doesn't seem important enough to take the extra 15 minutes to walk to the shop, and you just throw it in the bin with the intention of telling the shop the next time you're in there. Some thoughts will disappear after you've had them, whilst others are more significant and can be delayed until your set time. Whatever the case may be, it's much better to have set times in the day to worry about issues and problems than constantly dealing with them throughout the day when you have other things to deal with.

Lastly, establishing a set time to worry about issues allows you to spend the rest of your time not thinking about those issues and being more productive. Trigger thoughts don't lead to negative symptoms or the amount of these thoughts; it's the time you spend concentrating on them, the attention you give them, and the constant train of questions you ask yourself about. When you establish a clear schedule as to when you can worry about things, it shows you that you are the one in control and thus stops you from being anxious or stressed over it.

Reprogram Your Brain to Concentrate on Certain Things Only

For those who find it hard to cope with overthinking, it can be easy to become scared of these trigger thoughts. Feeling as though you have no control over your thoughts can make you want to avoid having them. However, you cannot control your trigger thoughts, nor can you stop having them, and if you avoid having them, then you will never be successful in managing them and enjoying all the possibilities and opportunities that life throws your way. If you want to drive a car, you must practice driving.

After reading all of this, are you ready to start? Great! The best thing to do is start giving yourself small tasks each day that will set off trigger thoughts, and practice how to delay them until a set time that you give yourself. This will help you develop the skills that allow you to push aside those trigger thoughts until you are ready, showing yourself that the only one in control is yourself. Remember, you will not be successful the first time and won't be successful every time, but if you want to drive that car, you need to get behind the wheel and start the engine.

Some people find this technique difficult to start. If this is the case for you, then you should look into attention training which will help you turn your thoughts no matter what the trigger thoughts or outside stimuli are.

Practice the following methods for ten minutes every day:

> *Go to a place where you can hear three or more separate sounds at the same time. This could be children playing, traffic sounds, and birdsong. The types of sounds don't matter, although it is more beneficial if the sounds are at different points to where you are (i.e., children playing are closer, whereas traffic sounds are farther away).*
>
> *Next, concentrate on one sound, such as the birdsong. Try and hold this for ten seconds,*

then move on to the sound of traffic for ten seconds, and then move on to the sounds of children playing for another ten seconds. You can use a timer if you need to.

Continue switching between these sounds for two minutes. After this time is up, do it again, but instead of holding your concentration on each sound for ten seconds, do it for three seconds each.

As you continue to practice and become better at it, you learn how to shift your attention from one sound to another. This can then be applied to things you know will trigger you and proves you can shift your attention from something negative to something that is much more beneficial.

Another extremely useful method is known as the windowpane technique and, just as the method mentioned above, clearly shows you that you are in control of your thoughts alone.

Take a pen with ink that can be easily wiped off and write a sentence on a window that you know will trigger you. It could be anything, like 'what if my date doesn't like me?" "what if I fail my exams?" or even "what if no one wants to hear my ideas?"

Look at the window and pay attention to what you can see beyond it – the houses, the trees, the clouds in the sky, the people walking by. Then look back at the words you've written on the window. Now shift your attention back to the view outside.

This technique aims to illustrate that you have the power to shift your focus and that you are in command of what you pay attention to. When you practice this, you will discover that while the words, i.e., the trigger thought, are still there, you are the one that controls what attention you give them; you can choose to focus all your attention on the trigger thought or focus on the world outside the trigger thought.

Why Do We Overthink At All?

Everyone is guilty of overthinking at times, but some overthink too much. Many of these people could actually have depression or anxiety, although not everyone. In some cases, it is pathological, according to psychologists, although for most, it is just overthinking. Some equate overthinking with problem-solving, but this just causes people to go around and around in a circle but never fix it.

Overthinking originates from a fear of the unknown. When we are uncertain of something, we try to fix it in our minds. For example, you have an argument with your manager. You then begin to worry about whether you are going to get fired. How can you pay your rent if you don't have a job? Will they give you a bad reference if you apply somewhere else? Will anyone hire me in my industry without a good recommendation?

Your Mind's Process

How your mind processes overthinking is still shrouded in mystery to experts, although it is theorized that it stimulates the same area of the brain that deals with stress and being scared, known as the amygdala. This consists of two clusters of cells near the base of the brain and is associated with defining and regulating emotions. All areas of thinking originate in the cerebral cortex, the part that replays memories. However, the amygdala cluster cells are stimulated if you are constantly overthinking something, such as an argument, a letter, or an obstacle. When this happens, your emotions are heightened, your heart races, and your muscles can become tense.

The more you focus on something, the more you're actually training your mind to focus on it. In turn, you stimulate the amygdala section of your brain, which releases more stress and emotions. When you do this, you're endangering yourself by putting yourself in a horrible cycle and possibly developing depression and anxiety.

Deceive Your Mind

Think of overthinking as a hoover – you get sucked into it. Overthinking a situation or issue takes you away from your surroundings and the things you want to do. However, there are ways to conquer this horrible pattern and take back control. You can't do this by demanding yourself not to think certain thoughts – your mind will simply focus more on those thoughts instead. The best thing to do in this situation is to substitute those thoughts with others.

Imagine if someone tells you to not think about blue monkeys. Is your mind going to do what that person says and never think of blue monkeys? Of course not! Your brain will instantly show you a bunch of blue monkeys dancing across your mind. To not think about blue monkeys, you need to think about green cats. Viola! There are no blue monkeys in your head now.

Tricking your mind into not focusing on something at that moment can be hugely rewarding. Let's say you're at work and your colleague tells you something worrying but nothing that's life or death. You need to push those worries aside until the time that you have set for this and then allow yourself to think about it if it warrants it. Having plans such as this helps you get back to work and deal with things that have to be dealt with, as well as not putting your mental health at risk.

Find Your Way Out

When you are aware that you are overthinking, you've actually taken the first step in finding your way out of there. There are several ways which can help you. First, understand that you're overthinking and address how you're feeling. If you're feeling uneasy, maybe take a quick walk or jog down the street. Pay attention to your surroundings, focus on your breathing, and shift your focus. When you recognize that your brain is overthinking, you need to divert its attention elsewhere instead of focusing on the situation or problem that causes you stress and anxiety.

You have to remember that not every problem can be fixed, and it's not always your job to fix it. Other people have responsibilities. If you are faced with a problem, then ask yourself, "is this really my problem to solve?" If you're trying to get more customers into the shop, it's only your problem if you're in charge of that particular responsibility. If you're a cashier, it's not your responsibility. If you're not a doctor, it's not down to you to save that person bleeding on the operating table.

Remember, you can't change the way your brain thinks in 24 hours. It takes time, patience, and dedication. But it can be done, and you're the only one who can do it.

Another popular method is by doing something kind for someone. Everyone is going through a struggle of some sort, but not everyone is open about it. When you do something kind for someone else, whether a family member, a friend, a colleague or even a stranger, you actually help yourself; maybe you could pick up some groceries for your neighbor who's just had a c-section or babysit a friend's children while she's going through a divorce. When you do something nice, you not only concentrate on that instead of your trigger thoughts, but you realize that you have the ability to change someone's day for the better, which is powerful.

Remember all the successes that you have had throughout your life. When your brain has gone into overdrive, and you're dwelling on negativity, take a few moments and thank yourself for all your accomplishments. Take a pen and write down ten positive things that have happened to you in the last few weeks and your part in them.

Accomplishments do not have to be huge. Perhaps you cleaned out your closet. Perhaps you sorted out your fridge. Maybe you wrote a budget, and you stuck to it. Maybe you read the book you got for your birthday. Maybe you took a box of items to the charity shop. The size or importance of these successes do not matter – what's important is that they happened. And when you look at them on paper or screen, it's amazing to see how many of them there actually are!

If you find yourself overthinking and it feels overwhelming, go back to that list and read it aloud. Or you may want to continue adding new accomplishments to that list as you go on. They remind you of the good things in life and the only things you should be focusing on.

Recognize and Welcome the Things You Are Scared Of

It's a fact of life that everyone is scared of something. When we are scared, we lose control. Everyone will lose control of something in their lives. Although it is scary, we must recognize and embrace it in order to stop overthinking. Experts state that when you accept these fears, your mental health actually gets better.

It is important to remember that embracing the things you fear is a very hard task, and success doesn't come overnight. The best way to start is to seek out smaller changes that will allow you to meet these opportunities head-on. This could be standing your ground with an argumentative colleague or traveling overseas alone.

Don't worry about overcoming them on your first try. Just remember to never stop taking small steps forward each time, and over time when you look back, you will amaze yourself with how far you have come.

Chapter Six:
Training to Be Confident

Sometimes it feels as though everyone has the self-confidence you wish you had yourself. However, if you knew them, then you may be surprised to discover that they suffer from doubting themselves just as you do.

So, what makes them different from you?

Well, they have understood and accepted that self-confidence isn't a possession; it is something you form for yourself. They have realized and embraced that being certain of achieving something when focused doesn't simply make one confident – instead, they understand it originates deep within you.

However, just because you are building up your confidence doesn't mean that you will fix every problem that runs your way. It's perfectly normal to experience negative or bad moments in life. It doesn't mean that you don't doubt yourself at times. As you build up confidence, you come to realize and accept that you won't know everything. Instead, it's about being sure that you will be able to deal with every experience and learn from it.

Educating yourself on how to be confident is an important tool that will help you experience the best in life. There will be times that you will have to rely on being confident, especially the moments when you are facing tough challenges and just want to huddle up into a small ball and cry.

If you are in a role where you have to lead others, then being confident is a must. No one will respect anyone in authority who is seen as being unconfident. How can you assemble a fantastic crew and guide them to accomplish great things together without confidence?

Even if you aren't a leader, being confident in yourself and your abilities is essential to being part of a team. This includes a variety of positions, such as a customer service agent dealing with unhappy customers, a salesperson negotiating with potential clients, or even when you are dealing with company management. When you are confident, you form relationships that can help improve the company you work for.

Also, these tools will help you form personal and romantic relationships outside the workplace. People are attracted to confident people, and it also helps you form healthy partnerships through communication and dealing with conflicts.

The Aspects of Being Confident

If you are ready to learn how to improve your self-confidence, then you have to be ready to change your state of mind. Your emotions are dictated by how you view and feel about yourself and can change throughout the day. However, don't feel scared, as you can alter your state of mind providing you know how to do it. Read on to discover the main aspects of being confident and how to implement them in your day-to-day life.

Body Language

Your body speaks for itself, and others around you can instantly read you without you opening your mouth. When you learn to be more confident, you will discover that your body will convey more than your words ever will. Think back on a time when you met someone you thought was confident; most likely, you thought they were confident prior to them talking. This is probably due to their body language. They looked you in the eye, kept their back straight, and shook your hand with a firm grip. Now think about your body and how you move it. Is your back straight? Do you make eye contact? Is your breathing steady? Keeping your head down, bad posture, and even fast, shallow breaths can make you feel less assured about yourself, which others around you pick up on. It is within your ability to change what your body tells others.

Being Positive

Positive thinking can show up in numerous ways. You start initially by changing how you view situations. It's easy to say, 'oh, this is going to go really bad.' Instead, look at all the positive outcomes. Don't think of all the ways you could screw up your next presentation; think of all the things that you will get right and how your colleagues will react to it. Whatever you concentrate on will come true, and this is especially true when it comes to your mindset. Replace all negative mantras with positive ones. When you shift your mindset from negative to positive, both within your mind and outside of it, you are able to shift how opportunities present themselves and ultimately make a positive outcome for your life.

Controlling Your Emotions

Humans experience a variety of feelings and emotions. This is what separates us from most animals. It's normal and healthy to experience them all, including joy, sadness, fear, anger, and determination. However, allowing them to dictate your life and all the experiences that come with it is not healthy. Confidence means that you have control over your emotions. No one is born with confidence; it's something that you form yourself over the years. When you learn how to build your confidence, you learn that whatever goal you set yourself, you can achieve it. Confidence is just like all emotions – you feel it, and you are in control of it.

A Learning Mindset

It is commonly believed that you are only confident once you have achieved something great. However, this couldn't be further away from the truth. You don't have to be the CEO of an international company, a lawyer with a high win percentage, or the doctor that everyone calls in an emergency to be confident. If you think this, then you are placing strict limitations on yourself. Achievements such as those mentioned are outside accomplishments, but they don't affect how you feel – that originates from inside you. When you are confident in yourself, you know that if and when you run into obstacles, you can deal with them and carry on instead of just giving up. When you begin to take the necessary steps in order to build your confidence, you will start to experience your attitude solidifying. You need to have a mindset focused on learning and believe you can be more confident.

Learning the Ways to Build Confidence

When you look at these three aspects, you will notice that they have a common theme – controlling your emotions. You must shift your mindset and say to yourself, "I will be more confident. To do this, you must be certain in yourself that you have the ability to be confident. It's easier to say this than to do it, at least in the beginning, but there are many steps that will allow you to get to where you want to be.

i. Love Yourself

You need to love yourself, warts and all, to feel genuinely confident in yourself. Once you have embraced the love, you will be confident in yourself regardless of what you experience in your life since that love originates from within you, not outward of you.

So, how do you fall in love with yourself? Look inside you. What values do you have? Take pride in those. What are your strengths? Take pride in them. What weaknesses do you have? Embrace those. Weaknesses are great in the fact that they show you areas you can improve on. Look at yourself as a whole. All these parts make you unique; no one else on Earth is like you. It's normal to doubt yourself, but remember to love every part of you no matter what.

ii. Overcome Any Limitations

When you don't love yourself, you start placing limitations on your beliefs and capabilities, or even what type of people you should be in a relationship with. When this happens, it causes you to harm yourself and solidify those thoughts. To achieve complete confidence in yourself, you need to conquer those beliefs.

So, how do we do this? First, take a good look at yourself and ask what thoughts are limiting your confidence. It tends to be the experiences in life that will connect how we feel about ourselves with negative emotions such as stress, anxiety, and self-doubt. When you experience these, they are your mind trying to put limitations on you. Replace them with positivity by imagining yourself in ideal situations with those limitations removed, and remind yourself that limitations are just stops along the way, not the end of the road.

iii. Unite Confidence with Goals

Why is it important for you to learn how to be more confident? Do you have a role at work that requires you to deal with lots of people? Are you part of a team, or perhaps the leader of a team where you need to show others strong levels of confidence? Are you interested in starting a relationship with someone and want to attract them?

When you want to achieve something, it is vital that you understand why you want to achieve it. Identifying this purpose allows you to use it as a foundation for building up confidence.

iv. Changing Your Body Language

The best way to start building up your confidence is to change how your body language. Keep your back straight when you talk to others. Keep your shoulders back and thrust your chest out a little more. Keep your breathing steady and deep. Keep your strides full of strength and purpose when you walk and be vigorous. Your mind will quickly follow when your body portrays an air of confidence.

The next time you're out, look at the people around you and pay attention to those with who you associate with a strong sense of confidence. How someone moves, the way they sit, and the way they fill up the room tells you a lot about how they interact with situations. You can then apply these to your own body and mindset.

v. Embrace the Things You Have Achieved

Just as changing the way you physically present yourself to others can help you feel more confident, embracing the things you have achieved even when you feel as though you are not worthy of those things can do exactly the same thing. Many of your colleagues who achieve great things at work do so because they embrace the things they achieved and do it right at the best time.

If you have played a role in a team that achieved something positive – maybe a new client or completed a tricky project – then it's perfectly normal to say so to your boss, CEO, or team leader. You don't have to sound conceited; a straightforward and realistic way is all that is needed. Not only will your boss view you differently, but you will do the same!

vi. Determine Your Most Important Needs

A good way of starting to learn how to build up your self-confidence is to figure out what is your most important need. This need, in particular, will drive you in life and impact all the choices you make throughout your life, as well as your confidence levels. If your most important need is certainty, then you may not feel confident in situations you are unfamiliar with. If your most important need is love, then you may not feel complete or worthy unless you are in a relationship. Look at yourself and your goals, and determine your most important need and the possible ways it affects your confidence.

vii. Work on How You Talk to Yourself

The way you talk to yourself will play a big part in the strengthening of your self-esteem and self-confidence levels, as well as the emotions you feel and project to the world.

Determine the way you talk to yourself. Do you ask yourself things such as, 'why are you not successful?', 'why can't you be like so-and-so?' or 'why are you so stupid?'

If you do, you are sabotaging yourself. Is it right for other people to talk to you the same way? No, it isn't. It's abusive, damaging, and limiting. Would you say those same things to someone else? Absolutely not. So why would you do the same to yourself?

Change the questions you ask yourself. 'What is a better use of my time than playing games on the computer?' 'What use is it to concentrate on my weaknesses instead of my strengths?', or even 'what do I need to work on to be a better leader/team player?' You get the right answers to the right questions.

viii.   Change the Way You Look at Things

There are times when everyone feels disheartened or depressed over something. When this happens, you don't have to stop. Just change the way you look at things. When you fail and get frustrated, you create a foundation that will allow you to look back and understand where you went wrong and live the life you want. Failures are not a sign for you to give up; they are a great teaching opportunity. Concentrate on the positive things about each situation, and accept them for what they are. You'll come to learn that you don't have to be scared of failing and become more confident because of it.

ix. Be Thankful

When you are thankful for what you have, you will become much happier. It is at this time when all your fears dissipate, and your life becomes rich and plentiful. Don't fear getting old – your body is more than just an object or a means to someone else's end. It is part of you, and it is beautiful and strong and has taken you to this moment.

It is important to be thankful for what you have right at this time instead of worrying about the things you don't have. So, you don't have five-hundred-dollar shoes on your feet at this time. Does it really matter? You have shoes in your closet that look good, and do what they are meant to – protect your feet from harm when you leave the house. So, what if you don't have a million-dollar house in the best part of town? You have a roof over your and your family's head, and that is important.

You need to change how you look at things and situations to stop looking at life in a way that only encourages negativity.

x. Pose of Power!

A good way of increasing your confidence levels is to reach and embrace the power within you. Everyone is strong, yet there are times when you forget just how strong you really are. You can find your strength by connecting it with a power pose. There are many poses which you can use – in yoga, the warrior move is an extremely popular one, or by folding your arms over your chest, hands on your hips, or defiantly raising your chin – but the most important aspect of this method is to find something that feels right to you. It should connect you to the inner most part of yourself, where your strength originates, and bring it out for everyone to see.

xi. Recall All the Successes You've Had Previously

Even when you feel that you've hit rock bottom, there is one technique that can make you feel confident about yourself; recalling all your past successes. For example, you need to make a presentation to the most important clients in your company's career – getting this client means the failure or success for your company – and you're scared of not landing them. Instead of thinking about all the things that could potentially go wrong, look back at all the clients you have landed. What's different about them? Absolutely nothing in reality. Think back to the ways you got them to sign on the dotted line – they wouldn't have done that if they weren't confident in your capabilities. They signed because they had confidence in what you were saying. Recalling these experiences will help reprogram your mind to think of new situations in more positive terms and ultimately improve your confidence.

xii. Visualize the Goals You Want to Achieve

When you use positive visualization techniques, you are using a method that helps you form a strong sense of confidence. It's a simple technique – you visualize the goals you want to achieve over and over and over again. When you do this, your brain starts to think it's already occurred. This means that your mind knows it can do this when the opportunity arrives – such as asking someone out on a date, asking for a promotion, etc. This is what being confident is. Think of something, see yourself achieving it, and sweep away any negative thoughts that will taint it. You reap what you sow.

xiii. Eye Contact Goes a Long Way

It can feel uncomfortable maintaining eye contact with someone else if you are not used to it, but doing so can make a world of difference. Many people find that even if they don't feel confident making eye contact at first, the more they do it the easier it becomes over time. When you maintain eye contact with someone, you connect with them, and this builds trust and confidence with each other, allowing you to create long-lasting relationships. Just remember to use the eighty-twenty rule: maintain eye contact with someone for eighty percent of the time, then twenty percent somewhere else; otherwise, the other person may feel intimidated and uncomfortable.

xiv. Establish Healthy Practices

It has been proven that when you implement a healthy routine, you can connect with the power inside you. You can benefit from many healthy practices, such as meditation and mindfulness, which are relaxing, calming, and reduce stress and anxiety. Incantations are a fantastic way of using your voice to establish goals and objectives. Others like to establish a workout routine, jogging, swimming, and walking the dog, all of which can clear your head for the day and has benefits for the body. It is these routines and others that can help you start the day off right by integrating positivity and the belief in yourself.

xv. Surround Yourself with Positive People

When you are learning how to be more confident, it can feel as though you're trying to push a boulder up the side of a very steep hill. It gets harder and more discouraging if the people around you are not providing the support and encouragement you need.

It is important to surround yourself with people who love you, want the best for you and will motivate you to keep going even when you don't feel as if you can. When you surround yourself with positivity, you attract positivity.

If you have no one in your life you feel will give you the support you need, there are others you can turn to. Life coaches, mentors, advisors, and even support groups are all out there to give you support and encourage you to overcome challenges.

xvi.   Caring for Your Brain

It isn't enough just to surround yourself with positive people; you need to maintain your brain. What do you read? What do you watch? Read books on people who have overcome challenges and hurdles to succeed. Watch programs about how people have gone from rags to riches. Scroll through the internet and seek motivational quotes that resonate with you.

Educate yourself on topics that will help you succeed. These could be things like learning marketing strategies, learning a new language, how to manage your finances, and even how to overcome your fears.

As you feed your brain with only positive things, you will reprogram it to know that you can do whatever you set out to do because you possess all the necessary skills for success.

xvii. Invest Time in a New Talent

It's perfectly normal to feel anxious or scared. But when you have faith in yourself, you start to understand that those feelings are ways your brain is telling you to be more active, to not stop or run away. You can conquer this feeling of being terrified by investing time in establishing new talent.

You can choose anything you like – such as playing an instrument, learning how to build a computer from scratch, or learning a new language – it doesn't really matter. Maybe something that you've always wanted to try. But when you do learn this new skill, you will discover that you are more confident in accomplishing tasks that you set yourself and maintaining discipline.

If that isn't enough, scientists have proven that the more our brains learn, the more dopamine is released. This hormone is commonly referred to as the reward molecule. As you learn, the brain creates fresh neural connections that benefit you.

xviii. Learn to Live Now

One of the hardest areas to be more confident in is relationships. If you have suffered abuse, gaslighting, been cheated on, or lied to in a relationship, it makes it harder to form new and healthy relationships. In order to not feel hurt or pain again, we try to not express our emotions, which then strains the relationship, and in turn causes you to constantly give yourself stress. Remember, no two people are the same, and no two relationships will be the same either. Learn to live in the now and free yourself of pain from the past and doubts about the future.

Chapter Seven:
Practicing with Purpose

There aren't many who achieved success in the field of business without self-confidence. However, many of these people, including CEOS, will experience moments of self-doubt about whether they can overcome the challenges they face. Feelings of self-doubts are just like any other emotion. It's normal, but they don't have to overwhelm you.

When you have confidence, you feel secure. When you feel secure, you experience positive emotions. When you feel positive emotions, the results tend to be better. Everyone experiences insecurities at some point in their lives, even the most confident person you've ever met. The first step in overcoming them is to look hard at your strengths and weaknesses, embrace them, and then work on them.

Think of an area that you want to work on. Once you have decided on one, start investing time and dedication to it. When you don't think you have the skills to complete a particular project, it's easy to say, 'I give up' and walk away. But truth is you only fail when you walk away. In fact, hard work and dedication succeeds where talent fails.

If you have to give a presentation to a room full of strangers and you're scared of messing up, start practicing what you need to say instead of passing the task on to someone else. You can do this at home or even in front of a mirror, but it should be somewhere you feel comfortable. Practice doesn't necessarily make perfect, despite what the old saying says, but it will help you improve and move in the right direction the more you try. If you can, practice it in front of someone you trust who can give you honest feedback. People with confidence understand that practicing and learning lead to better results and that they don't know everything. They understand that when they need help, they can always ask for it. This is what confidence is – to admit to needing support when required.

As such, do not let the fear of what others may think of you stop you from doing what needs to be done. It's easy enough to get in your own head, to feel judged by friends and colleagues. However, when you concentrate on the steps that lead you to success, you simply don't have time to think about how others perceive you. In fact, the whole concept of confidence is not necessary anymore. What is important is purpose.

Ask for feedback when you require it. If you are feeling unconfident about your work, don't hesitate to ask someone you trust for their feedback. Having someone validate your work can greatly boost your confidence, especially if it comes from someone you trust and admire. However, this person must provide honest, constructive feedback. If a person simply says good things to get you to go away or even to make you feel confident, it wouldn't really help you as it doesn't allow you to identify your mistakes and improve on them.

Risks Are Good

Everyone has their own strengths and weaknesses, and tend to only play to their strengths as much as possible. However, doing so excessively stops you from taking risks, in turn ending up limiting you. Risks allow you to face obstacles and as you find ways of overcoming them, you grow and improve in the process. You never know what you can achieve until you try, after all.

For some, failing is a fantastic experience. It gives you a chance to learn something. So, you couldn't get over that boulder this way; what happens if you try from a different angle?

It's perfectly natural not to be instantly good at something the first time you try it. But in order to be successful, you need to persevere and try again, but try better. You must take that leap of faith and keep going until you overcome it.

Find someone, such as a friend, mentor, or supervisor at work, to walk you through a new challenge and support you as you grow these skills. You'd be surprised at how far you go with that leap of faith.

Aspects to Remember

- *It is important to be completely open about your strengths and your weaknesses.*
- *Carry on practicing new skills.*

- *Learn to seize all opportunities that allow you to learn and grow.*
- *Ask for help or guidance when you need it, and don't feel guilty for it.*
- *Stop thinking about what other people think about you.*
- *Only concentrate on yourself and what you bring to the table without comparing yourself to others.*

Chapter Eight:
The Key to Increasing Your Confidence

It's normal to want to compare yourself to the people that are around you. It is also very common to feel inadequate compared to others when doing this.

However, it is important to remember that everyone is different. Just as you have strengths and weaknesses, so do they. Their personality is different from yours; therefore, their experiences and opportunities will differ from those that come your way.

It is vital that you not only accept this but learn from your strengths and weaknesses. The things that you are strong and excel at are the things that can help drive you forward. However, your weaknesses are not what will stop you but things you need to work on, improve at, and learn from.

Think about your first day at school. Did you know all your ABCs and instantly know the entire periodic table? Of course not. You learn through study, practice, and research, with help from teachers.

You need to know what your strengths are and what weaknesses you need to work on. Most people don't know this, but it will change everything once you do.

Understanding What You're Strong At

Your biggest strength is the one thing you do well at. It's a thing that you can do without thinking. It could be writing, cooking, teaching, drawing – absolutely anything.

A great way of recognizing your strengths is by writing a list of attributes that you have. Now rearrange them from one to five, with one being the top and most dominant attribute and the fifth as the least likely to symbolize you.

Now you know what your main strengths are, you can utilize them.

Understanding What Your Weaknesses Are

Knowing what weaknesses you possess is just as important as your strengths. When we feel as if we are weak at something, it limits us. It can even stop us. However, it is important to understand that our weaknesses are just as valuable as our strengths. This is because we can recognize the areas that we can improve on. Everyone has weaknesses, but only a few people will actually have the courage and confidence to work on them.

Just as with your strengths, write your weakest attributes on a piece of paper and rearrange them in order. Number one should be your most dominant weakness, whilst the fifth should be the one that least represents you.

Now you know what your weaknesses are, you can start working on them.

These are the two simplest exercises that you can do to determine your strengths and weaknesses. If you want more in-depth results, there are some fantastic exercises you can find on the internet.

Why Is Understanding My Strengths and Weaknesses Important?

Many people lose their confidence when they keep trying and get the same result: failure. When you understand your strengths and weaknesses, you learn more about yourself than what you thought you knew.

When you recognize these strengths and weaknesses, it allows you to step ahead. For example, if you know you are good at budgeting, then you may decide on a career in finance or accounting. Many people stick to careers that they know they're good at, which helps with their confidence.

In addition, it gives you the opportunity for growth. If you know you're good at something, you know you can reach the next level. This allows you to grow and succeed.

When you recognize your own personal weaknesses, it's like looking in a mirror and seeing who is stopping you from achieving what you want to achieve. You can then find the right way to lessen their grip and free yourself completely.

Is It Better to Concentrate Only on My Strengths or Just My Weak Points?

It's a common question people ask if they are unsure what areas to work on. For the most part, concentrating on your strengths will have better results for you. These are the areas that you know you excel at, things you don't have to concentrate on as much.

When you focus on your strengths, you are really working on how to attain new experiences and opportunities. You stop concentrating on the negative things, leaving you with more time and energy to focus on your strengths.

However, you must work on the things you are weak at as it will allow you to grow. You can't make your weaknesses disappear, and you can't improve them simply overnight, but if you make some changes, you can improve it. Or you find ways to get around them. In turn, your confidence will improve, and you will have better opportunities and experiences.

For example, you need to hold an event. You're not particularly good at creating beautiful invitations, but you are fantastic at organizing what needs to be done. Instead of wasting time on creating invitations that won't be good enough, you set someone who is creative to do them. It can be as simple as that. You know exactly what your weak areas are, but instead of fretting over them, you deal with them.

When you know your strong and weak points, you give yourself the gift of growth and development.

Chapter Nine:
Looking the Part

It can often seem that confidence is somewhat like chasing a dream. If you want to be successful, you need confidence, but grabbing it and holding onto it can be hard. Some people just seem to ooze confidence at every turn, but for the majority, it can be daunting and hard to attain, particularly if you are in uncomfortable situations.

Before you do anything, you need to remember that millions of other people are just like you. It is also important to remember that looking confident outwards is just as important as feeling confident within. If you look and act confident even if you don't really feel that way, it will still allow others to have confidence in you, which in turn helps boost your confidence levels.

Ways to Appear More Confident

i. Have Good Posture

Standing up straight and tall, with your shoulders back, can make you fill a room. Not only will this give you better back support and make it easier to breathe, but it will also give you the appearance of being confident to those around you. People often equate bad posture, such as slouching, with not being confident or assured about themselves. You can also practice power poses – although they may seem silly, research has shown them to help raise confidence levels, so they could be a great thing to do before entering a room.

ii. Maintaining Eye Contact

Start working on your eye contact if you want to look like you're dripping with confidence. Whenever you are talking with someone, always look them in the eye. If you're with several others, then ensure that you look at each of them. If you are addressing a room full of people, it is beneficial for you to look at members of the crowd in the eye. Also, if someone is talking to you, then keep looking at them. If you drop your eye, then it makes you look uncertain or nervous. However, do not stare at people one hundred percent of the time as this can make them feel intimidated – it is important to look at other people or areas around twenty percent of the time.

iii. Stop Fidgeting

When you fidget, it illustrates to other people that you are not as confident as you think you are. You fidget differently; for some, it is constantly waving their hands as they speak, while for others, it manifests in their leg constantly moving up and down. Some will nod continuously, others will move from one leg to the other, and some will lick their lips. To convey an air of confidence, you need to stop moving. Stand up straight. Keep your hands and feet still. Don't lick your lips or play with your hair. The only time you need to move is when it is necessary. If you are someone who fidgets a lot, this can be hard to do, but with some practice, you can work on it. If you are uncertain of your fidgeting habits, you could ask someone you trust to tell you.

iv. Talk Concisely

Another way of showing that you lack confidence in yourself is by speaking in low tones or by talking fast. It also allows you to say things you didn't want to say or just ramble on with things that don't have anything to do with the topic. In this case, you need to speak concisely and take your time. Don't rush the things you want to say. Think about the words you use. When you do this, the people you communicate with will believe you are confident. You can do this with a little practice, and it is easier to pick up than you may first think.

v. Be Silent.

You know the old saying – silence is golden. It's perfectly acceptable to be silent in many situations. Some wrongly believe that silences are awkward and signs of a terrible conversation. However, research shows that being silent is a vital tool in social situations. You can be silent after making a point, as this helps drive the point home. You can be silent to indicate to the other person that they should speak or illustrate your listening abilities. Silences are tools to show consideration and confidence in how you talk.

vi. Use Your Hands

Fidgeting is not good, but how you move your hands can greatly impact how others feel that you are confident. You don't have to flail them about in front of the other person's face, but a few intentional and careful gestures can drive home your point. Don't hide your hands behind your back or in your pockets. You can also use your hands to touch the other person, such as on the shoulder or arm, but only if the situation calls for it.

vii.   Walk the Walk

When you enter a room, you need to fill it. When you walk around the room, you need to use brisk strides that convey power and confidence. And when you exit the room, you do it with the same assuredness. To appear confident, keep your spine straight as you walk with long and certain strides. You don't need to be a fast walker. Slow down a little and show that you're not in a rush. You appear more confident when you walk this way, and everyone around you will feel it.

What makes looking confident so great is that after a while, you reprogram your mind into believing that you are confident. Just as with good conversation and body language, all these aspects can be easily achieved with a little practice. If you practice looking as though you are confident, then it will come easily to you in time.

Chapter Ten:
Balancing between Confidence and Overconfidence

As we have seen, being confident is great as it opens up new opportunities and experiences. However, being overconfident is generally seen as a negative thing. As a result, it is important that you do not step over that very fine line.

Getting that balance of being confident enough without being overconfident makes a world of difference. However, many people are still uncertain as to what the difference is between the two terms, so it is important that we understand them.

What Are the Differences between Confidence and Overconfidence?

Confidence is the knowledge and understanding that while you may make mistakes along the way, you have the skills to overcome any challenge.

Overconfidence is where you take so much pride in yourself that you do not think you make mistakes and can do anything to the point of being arrogant.

It is perfectly healthy to be confident in your abilities – it is not bad to be certain about something you are doing.

Being overly confident to the point of arrogance is limiting. When you are arrogant about your abilities, you have an extreme belief that you cannot make any mistakes.

Think of all the times when you've seen someone show off – this is one of many examples of being arrogant. They are often rude, overly proud, and usually disrespectful to their team or colleagues. They are not respected, nor are they followed.

It is always better to be yourself. Don't pretend to be someone you aren't. You don't need to copy someone else or show off. In fact, this type of pretense can actually hurt you by undermining your existing confidence and cast you in a negative light to those who look to you for guidance or teamwork. People should always be comfortable enough to talk to you. When have you ever been comfortable talking to someone who is arrogant? You haven't. No one has.

When you talk to other people, all you need to do is say things matter-of-factly. This isn't rude; it's not arrogant – it's just facts. If you don't agree with what the other person says, you don't need to overreact by keeping silent or shouting to get your point across; you just have to tell them what you think, and agree to disagree if you can't come to an agreement.

It's Not Necessary to Compete with Others

You don't need to be hungry for competition to become confident. In fact, you don't need to win anything at all in order to be confident or successful, no matter what some people may claim.

Arrogant people see everything as a competition, thinking that being better than others help them feel confident. They don't see what they're doing as harmful. Everyone makes mistakes, and arrogant people pounce on the opportunity to exert their dominance over others.

Instead of only trying to dominate your competition, view it in a healthy way – an opportunity to better your skills and aid others along the way.

Hiding

As mentioned, you're only human, and humans make mistakes. It happens to even the best of us. Arrogant people see mistakes as only happening to other people, not themselves. Arrogant people see themselves as unfailing and don't listen to what others say. Arrogant people don't take responsibility for their actions but will take all the glory.

A confident person will understand that they make mistakes and, when they do, will take responsibility for it. They will listen to what other people have to say, correct their mistakes and view it all as a learning experience.

Keep an Open Mind

It's very easy to step over the line from confidence to overconfidence, especially when it's such a fine line. Most of us will not realize it when we do cross over it.

It can be hard to tell when we are being confident and when we are overly confident.

A good way of ensuring you're still on the right side is by talking to someone you trust to give you feedback on the things you say. However, you do need to be able to take constructive criticism, which not everyone is comfortable with.

Yet, if you keep an open mind, you can embrace the most significant points and work on what you need.

Offer Constructive Criticism

Most people want to improve themselves and their circumstances. When you are in a leadership role, you now have the opportunity of being able to help others and give guidance to them. This is an extremely powerful role as you can impact that person's view of themselves, and either push them to do better or stamp them into the ground.

Everyone has strengths and weaknesses, just like you. When you are in a position to offer criticism to someone else, do it from a place of respect. Be constructive, not destructive. Recall the times when you were struggling to improve yourself. Would you have preferred someone to give you help with respect and dignity or with arrogance and superiority?

Arrogant people will be destructive in their criticism. They will give off an air of superiority, poking at all the other person's flaws, ridiculing them for every single mistake they've ever made.

A confident person will be respectful, calm, and point out both their flaws and strengths to focus on.

You're Only in Competition with Yourself

A little competition never hurts anyone, according to the old saying. However, that is only when you're participating in it in a healthy way.

Competing with yourself is a healthy thing to do. You've made it to an employee of the month – woohoo! Now you want to make it two months in a row. That's great. You take the time to see what things you can improve on from the previous month and carry on with the things that you're great at. This is all good.

However, it is unhealthy when you look at what other people are doing and see what their results are like. Now you're competing against them. Jealously starts to raise its ugly head, and then you deliberately start sabotaging them to make yourself look and feel good. This is arrogance.

When it comes to competitions, only compete with yourself. You'll get fantastic results every time.

Appreciate Other People

An arrogant person will only think about themselves. They don't care about the achievements or contributions of others. This is not a great thing for anyone, including yourself.

When you are arrogant, the people surrounding you start to lose respect for you. They don't want to be around you, they don't want to communicate with you, and some will want you to fail.

If you are in a leadership role, you should want other people to respect and communicate with you. A good leader is a respected leader. When you don't recognize and appreciate what other people bring to the table, you'll soon discover no one will come back. People won't work with you.

People don't leave good jobs; they leave bad management. Do not neglect those around you. It will only harm you in the end.

Don't Rely on Yourself All the Time

Being independent is great, especially when you are able to complete tasks and overcome obstacles through your own efforts. However, relying on yourself always isn't as great as you think.

If you want to succeed, then the most significant tools you possess are the people around you. In business, you need to have a great team. Teams are made up of several people, all with fantastic resources and skills. Networking is a vital part of business, and the work of individuals makes for a successful project.

When you attempt to do everything by yourself, you're not showing yourself to be confident – you're showing that you're being arrogant. Appreciate every single person's contribution, including yourself, and work as a team. After all, there is no I in the team.

Be Perceptive

If you want to stick to the side of being confident and not arrogant, then you need to be able to take a good, hard look at yourself. You must always be aware of your own actions to ensure you don't stray from the path, since jumping from one side to the other can often happen without realizing it.

Think about the things you say and do, evaluate your thoughts and determine on which side they are all placed. This will help keep you from appearing as arrogant, and if you do end up being arrogant, it can help guide you back to the right side before you cause any more damage to yourself.

You will need to learn how to be honest with yourself, how to be genuine, and learn from your mistakes.

Mistakes Are Educational

Arrogance is like a nasty bully whispering dangerous and harmful things into your ear when the teacher isn't listening. It tells you things such as 'he failed because he's not good enough, but that won't happen to you because you're better than he is.'

The thing is, arrogance lies. He doesn't tell the truth. Everyone makes mistakes. No one is perfect. When you don't learn from your mistakes, you end up repeating them. You get disgruntled and discouraged, and instead of figuring out what you did wrong, you do the same thing over again only to get the same results. This is why so many people eventually give up.

It happens in every part of life – studies, careers, even relationships.

Educating yourself on where you went wrong increases your confidence to try again and succeed. This is true of learning from other people's mistakes. But an arrogant person will not see it as a learning experience that they can benefit from; for them, it's just something to ridicule others for.

Be Respectful

Being respectful can help you keep a healthy balance between being confident and being overly confident. No arrogant person is respectful of others. Humility is not a word in their dictionary.

Humility is the opposite of arrogance. Arrogance is confidence without respect or modesty. It is fantastic to succeed in your career, but when respect and modesty are not with it, you just appear as being arrogant.

If you want to remain confident but not arrogant, you should always be respectful and modest. When you are arrogant, you stop learning, you stop growing, and you aren't able to lead others or help them grow.

You Don't Need to Always Talk about Your Past Achievements

There is nothing wrong with taking pride in your accomplishments; you should celebrate them. They are a great way to encourage you to carry on and improve yourself. They are a reminder of where you've come from and push you to where you want to be.

However, you need to ensure they don't nurture arrogance within you. It is very easy to draw on these accomplishments and make you think that there is nothing else for you to achieve or that you are better than others because they don't have the same achievements as you do.

Accomplishments should be used to encourage you to do better, not make you think you have nothing else to learn or do. If you do, then you have stepped over the line of being arrogant.

Embrace the Mistakes

Mistakes are normal. Let me repeat that. *MISTAKES ARE NORMAL.*

But it is the way you use these mistakes that determine whether you are confident or arrogant.

An arrogant person doesn't believe that they can make mistakes, and it is always another person's fault. This leads to disrespecting and neglecting others and puts you in a bad light.

It is only in your best interest to accept and embrace your mistakes. When you make a mistake, you have the opportunity to evaluate where you went wrong, fix the issue, and be confident enough to try again without repeating them. An arrogant person will not only refuse to fix the problem but not even accept the issue in the first place.

Confident people will learn from every experience, both positive and negative. You cannot teach an arrogant person who refuses to learn.

Work on Your Communication Skills

As mentioned earlier, communication is essential if you want to succeed because no man is an island. Business is all about forming relationships with others – whether that be customer service reps, the finance team, marketing teams, secretaries, etc. What do they all have in common? You need to communicate with them.

We can't do everything ourselves, nor should we. We must communicate with others to discuss plans, ideas, mistakes, etc. We need to listen to the thoughts and ideas of others.

We need to communicate.

Not only do we need to push ourselves to communicate, but even more than that, we need to learn how to express ourselves. The art of delivery can make or break a conversation. Learning how to turn your thoughts and intentions into words is a skill that you need in every aspect of your life.

After all, no one wants to work with someone with bad interpersonal skills. Therefore, we need to be able to talk, listen, and form relationships with others, even if we don't always agree with what they say. We must recognize what everyone brings to the table to enjoy the bounty of success. Once you're able to bring all these factors together and take your time to register what other people are trying to say, you'll be able to process the information calmly and confidently respond in a way that holds true to your expression and also does not offend anyone at the same time.

Conclusion

Being confident in a world that constantly strives to undermine you can be difficult. Society tries to make us all the same but yet demands that we all be successful. But how are you meant to feel confident in a world that doesn't allow you to be confident? How can you be confident in a relationship when all your previous relationships have been unhealthy or abusive? It's confusing and scary.

Confidence is an emotion. Just like anger, fear, love, hatred, determination, happiness, shame, guilt, and shyness, it is an emotion that we are all capable of feeling. Emotions are psychological states that greatly impact our lives, affecting everything from personal relationships, careers, studies, and everything in-between.

However, as with all other emotions, confidence is a feeling that can be taught and nurtured. We all learn to become confident at different rates. It comes from the experiences we go through from childhood. If we are lucky, we are taught by our parents how to be confident, to always learn from our mistakes, and not be afraid to try again until we have the outcomes we want. However, not everyone will have the privilege of having positive role models from an early age.

The great thing to understand is that confidence can be taught no matter how old you are—ten, twenty, thirty, forty, even a hundred years old. Brains can be reprogramed and taught, allowing you to seize every opportunity and experience the life you've always wanted.

A confident person knows that everyone makes mistakes. Confidence is where you can look at any situation, any obstacle, any mistake, learn from them, and deal with them. Confidence is the feeling that you can overcome any situation and thrive.

Confidence is yours.

Many times, low confidence stems from not having enough support. This is especially true when we are children. Being a child is tough as you have to conform to the rules and expectations of adults while at the same time figuring out who you are. Kids can be mean, and adults even meaner. Words hurt, actions can be damaging, and before you know it, you have low self-esteem and low confidence in yourself that you carry on through to your adult life.

As young adults, we are adapting to the pressures that society heaps upon our shoulders. Look this way, act this way, be successful, be humble, and be proud, all at the same time. Pressure can help us improve ourselves to encourage us to do better, yet it can be incredibly damaging at the same time. If you have not experienced the necessary support of loved ones or mentors, it can make you feel as though the whole world is on your shoulders and you're about to crumble from it.

However, when you are confident, you know that you can hold it, that your shoulders are strong enough to carry the weight of what is needed and to discard the things that aren't.

But how do you become confident when you feel as though you have nothing good enough to be confident about?

The first step is to recognize that confidence is just an emotion. It is inside you. You have the capability of feeling anger, to feel love, fear, drive, determination, happiness, and everything else. Therefore, you have the ability to feel confident. It's inside you, just like every other emotion.

You may not feel confident right now, but just by reading this book, you will recognize that you need help, guidance, and support to help you achieve confidence and self-esteem. This is a big deal. There are many unconfident people, as well as overly confident people, who never recognize that they need such guidance. Congratulate yourself as you have taken a long hard look at yourself, evaluated what you need, and have started on your journey to changing your life.

It doesn't matter if you're only looking to increase your confidence in one area. For example, if you aren't confident about your skills at work, you may feel as though you need constant guidance, and whenever you do ask for help, you feel like you're annoying or distracting those you work with. If you're unconfident in relationships, you may become overly attached and depend on the other person's attention and affection for affirmation of your status, leading to unhealthy interactions that build tension and causes stressful situations and could even end with awkward breakups.

The great thing about learning how to be more confident is that when you first start applying these techniques in one area, you soon apply them to other areas in your life. You learn how to share your opinions in meetings; you learn how to be independent and not overly attached in your romantic relationships. You learn how to say no to unreasonable requests and say no to the colleague who wants to thrust their workload onto you. And with the lessons you've learned over time, you become confident enough in yourself to share them with the people you recognize are struggling like you did before. You learn how to lead with confidence, and people will naturally follow you.

It is so easy to give up if you've constantly failed over and over again. After all, what's the point of continuing if you never seem to get anywhere? If you never feel as though you're going to win, you start acting as though you've already lost even before you begin. The cycle continues, spreading from one area of life to the others.

You must break this cycle if you genuinely want to change. You need the confidence to overcome failures, but to feel confident, it seems that you first need to be successful, to be a winner everyone loves. But to be a successful and well-loved winner, you must first have the confidence to do what it takes to succeed.

It's a conundrum, and a nasty one at that.

Even if you have already spent countless hours trying to figure out what has gone wrong, it feels as though you're always walking in circles. Without confidence, you're never going to get where you want to be, where you deserve to be.

However, this is where a lot of people go wrong. You do not need be successful before you start having the confidence to break out of this conundrum at all.

Think about some of the people you admire. It could be your boss. They ooze confidence; they're always on their phones talking to people, closing deals, and bringing in new clients. But pay attention. Do they really have hundreds of friends, or are they just colleagues, business associates, and clients? If they are married or in a relationship, how can you tell it's a happy and healthy one? Look at other people who have attained the success you crave. Some models still don't think they are beautiful enough, actors who turn to destructive substances because they can't handle the pressure of fame and fortune, and business owners who fear that even with billions in the bank, they aren't good enough until they double it.

You are not alone in your fears. You are not the only person who is unconfident in your skills and abilities.

It's a sad fact, but no one is perfect. And it's also a fact that confidence is not linked to wealth, fame, or outward success and achievements.

Now that we know confidence is not linked to anything external, we must recognize that confidence comes from within. Just because you're given a raise and promotion at work doesn't automatically make you confident in your skills to do that job to your boss's expectations.

Confidence comes from within us. It is a state of mind. It's the realization that you have the ability to overcome any obstacles along the way with the skills and ability to learn and adapt.

This book has covered every important aspect of your life and how you can manage your thought process and actions to give yourself a healthier outlook on life, those around you, and most importantly, yourself. If you utilize these tools and make them an integral part of your everyday life, you'll never have to worry about looking down or doubting yourself and your abilities again.

Always remember that if you don't take care of your mental well-being and how you perceive yourself, this will bleed into every other aspect of your life and create imbalance. So start today and remember that you decide how confident you want to be!

Resources

Booth, J. (n.d.). 8 Ways To Trick Yourself Into Feeling Confident, Even When You're Not. Insider. https://www.insider.com/how-to-be-more-confident-2018-1

Manson, M. (n.d.). The Only Way to Be Truly Confident in Yourself. Life Advice That Doesn't Suck. https://markmanson.net/how-to-be-confident

MasterClass. (n.d.). How to Be Confident: 8 Tips for Building Confidence. Masterclass. https://www.masterclass.com/articles/how-to-be-more-confident

Printed in Great Britain
by Amazon